SATYAJIT RAY'S FELUDA MYSTERIES

# THE CRIMINALS OF
# KAILASH

## ART: TAPAS GUHA
## SCRIPT: SUBHADRA SEN GUPTA

PUFFIN BOOKS

PUFFIN BOOKS

Published by the Penguin Group

Penguin Books India Pvt Ltd, 11 Community Centre, Panchsheel Park, New Delhi 110 017, India

Penguin Group (USA) Inc., 375 Hudson Street, New York, New York 10014, USA

Penguin Group (Canada), 90 Eglinton Avenue East, Suite 700, Toronto, Ontario, M4P 2Y3, Canada (a division of Pearson Penguin Canada Inc.)

Penguin Books Ltd, 80 Strand, London WC2R 0RL, England

Penguin Ireland, 25 St Stephen's Green, Dublin 2, Ireland (a division of Penguin Books Ltd)

Penguin Group (Australia), 250 Camberwell Road, Camberwell, Victoria 3124, Australia (a division of Pearson Australia Group Pty Ltd)

Penguin Group (NZ), 67 Apollo Drive, Rosedale, North Shore 0632, New Zealand (a division of Pearson New Zealand Ltd)

Penguin Group (South Africa) (Pty) Ltd, 24 Sturdee Avenue, Rosebank, Johannesburg 2196, South Africa

Penguin Books Ltd, Registered Offices: 80 Strand, London WC2R 0RL, England

This edition first published in Puffin by Penguin Books India 2011

Story copyright © The Estate of Satyajit Ray 2011
Text (in this comic) copyright © Subhadra Sen Gupta 2011
Illustrations © Tapas Guha 2011

A version of this comic book was first published as comic strips in *Telekids,* the children's supplement of the Telegraph, Kolkata. To read the latest page, go to the website www.telegraphindia.com and click on 'Telekids'.

ISBN 9780143331544

Printed at Manipal Press Ltd, Manipal

## FELUDA

Pradosh Chandra Mitter, professional detective. Feluda lives at
27 Rajani Sen Road, Ballygunje, Calcutta. Fans have gone looking for
his house and discovered that though the road is real, the houses
end at No. 26! He is called Felu at home and as he is Topshe's older
cousin, Topshe calls him Felu-da. He is 6 feet tall, good looking, very
athletic, does yoga, reads a lot and enjoys travelling. He has a .32 Colt
revolver and knows martial arts but usually solves his cases through
sheer brain power.

## TOPSHE

Tapesh Ranjan Mitter, Feluda's sidekick. Topshe is Dr. Watson
to Feluda's Sherlock Holmes and he narrates all the stories. He
is in his late teens and still going to school. Topshe loves reading,
especially Tintin and by carefully studying Feluda he is becoming
pretty good at detection.

## JATAYU

Lalmohan Ganguli, popular writer of thrillers under the pseudonym 'Jatayu'.
His fictional detective is called Prakhar Rudra. He owns a green Ambassador
car, driven by Haripada. He lives in Garpar, which is in fact the neighbourhood
where Satyajit Ray grew up. Jatayu gets scared very easily and his general
knowledge is rather confused, so Feluda often has to correct the
facts in his books!

THE MAGNIFICENT TEMPLES OF BHUBANESHWAR HAVE SEEN THE SETTING SUN FOR MANY CENTURIES.

THEIR BEAUTIFUL CARVINGS OF GODS, GODDESSES AND DEMONS HAVE FILLED US WITH AMAZEMENT.

THEY HAVE SURVIVED MANY STORMS BUT NOW THE TEMPLES FACE A VERY SERIOUS DANGER.

LATE ONE NIGHT, ART THIEVES ARE AT WORK AT THE RAJA RANI TEMPLE.

CHINK! CHINK!! CRACK!!!!

LET'S GO! WE HAVE TO CATCH THE NEXT TRAIN. THE BOSS IS WAITING FOR US IN CALCUTTA.

HERE YOU ARE MR SILVERSTEIN! THE SEVENTH CENTURY CARVING YOU WERE LOOKING FOR!

FANTASTIC! I HOPE IT'S GENUINE, MY FRIEND? YOU ARE ASKING FOR A VERY HIGH PRICE.

OF COURSE THIS IS THE REAL THING AND YOU ARE GETTING IT CHEAP. YOU CAN ASK ANY ART EXPERT IN CALCUTTA.

OH I WILL . . . I WILL . . . YOU CAN BE SURE OF THAT! MY FRIEND MR NAGARMAL HAS HIS ART GALLERY RIGHT HERE IN THIS HOTEL.

1

JUST MY LUCK! IT WAS THE FIRST DAY OF THE SUMMER HOLIDAYS AND IT BEGAN TO RAIN!

WE SHOULD PLAN A HOLIDAY TRIP, TOPSHE. WHERE DO YOU WANT TO GO?

HMMM . . . HOW ABOUT SOMEWHERE IN THE HILLS FELUDA?

HELLO! WHO'S COME IN THIS DOWNPOUR?

ding dong!!

SIDHU JETHA?! WHAT . . .

HOLD THIS UMBRELLA TAPESH AND ORDER HOT TEA FAST! WHERE'S FELU? CALL HIM. THIS IS URGENT!!

SOUNDS SERIOUS! WHAT'S UP . . . THEFT, KIDNAPPING, BLACKMAIL, MURDER?!

IT'S THE WORST CRIME OF ALL FELU! AND ONLY YOU CAN HELP!

OVER HOT TEA AND CRUNCHY PAKORAS, WE LISTEN TO SIDHU JETHA . . .

IT'S THE MURDER OF OUR CULTURAL HERITAGE! THAT'S WHAT HAS HAPPENED!

OUR GREATEST CULTURAL TREASURES ARE OUR TEMPLES AND THEY ARE IN DANGER.

I KNEW SIDHU JETHA WAS AN EXPERT ON INDIAN ART BUT . . .

!!??

HOW?? HAS THERE BEEN AN EARTHQUAKE?

DON'T BE SUCH AN IDIOT TAPESH! I'M TALKING OF SERIOUS CRIME HERE!

RIGHT! Y'MEAN. THE STONE CARVINGS IN THE TEMPLES . . . THEY ARE IN DANGER?

EXACTLY! DO YOU KNOW THEY ARE BREAKING OFF THE HEADS OF BEAUTIFUL STATUES TO SELL THEM TO TOURISTS?!

TODAY I WENT TO NAGARMAL'S ART GALLERY AT THE GRAND HOTEL TO SELL SOME PAINTINGS AND SAW SOMETHING SHOCKING!

NAGARMAL ART GALLERY

2

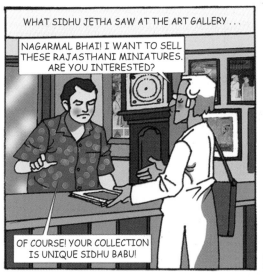

WHAT SIDHU JETHA SAW AT THE ART GALLERY . . .

NAGARMAL BHAI! I WANT TO SELL THESE RAJASTHANI MINIATURES. ARE YOU INTERESTED?

OF COURSE! YOUR COLLECTION IS UNIQUE SIDHU BABU!

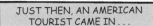

JUST THEN, AN AMERICAN TOURIST CAME IN . . .

HI NAGARMAL! I WANNA SHOW YA MY LATEST FIND!

I PAID TWO THOUSAND DOLLARS FOR THIS. TELL ME, IS IT REAL OR FAKE?

OH MY GOD!!! THAT'S A YAKSHI FROM THE RAJA RANI TEMPLE!!

THIS IS A GENUINE CARVING FROM ORISSA, SIR. VERY OLD INDEED!

AWESOME! PRETTY, ISN'T SHE?

CAN YOU IMAGINE! THE CROOKS CHISELLED IT OFF THE TEMPLE WALL! THEY MUST'VE BRIBED THE GUARDS. IT'LL SELL FOR TEN TIMES THAT PRICE ABROAD.

DO YOU KNOW THE AMERICAN'S NAME?

YES I DO. HE SAW MY PAINTINGS AND GAVE ME HIS VISITING CARD. HE'S LEAVING FOR KATHMANDU SOON. SO HURRY!

SOL SILVERSTEIN. IS HE STAYING AT THE GRAND?

YES. WILL YOU CALL HIM? I FORGOT TO ASK WHO SOLD THAT YAKSHI TO HIM.

WHAT'S A YAKSHI, SIDHU JETHA?

A YAKSHI IS A HEAVENLY WOMAN, PRETTIER THAN YOUR FILM STARS. READ SOME ART BOOKS, STUPID!

FELUDA IMMEDIATELY CALLS THE GRAND HOTEL . . .

MR SILVERSTEIN'S ROOM PLEASE. HE'S NOT IN? FINE . . . I'LL CALL LATER.

3

I READ IN THE NEXT MORNING'S NEWSPAPER . . .

'HEADLESS YAKSHI' THIEVES HAVE SLICED OFF THE HEAD OF A YAKSHI AT BHUBANESHWAR'S FAMOUS RAJA RANI TEMPLE. THE ARCHAEOLOGICAL SURVEY OF INDIA SAYS . . .

. . . AND THE GUARDS ARE MISSING . . . THEY MUST HAVE STOLEN IT AND SOLD IT TO SILVERSTEIN!

NOPE! THIS IS THE WORK OF A GANG OF EDUCATED MEN WHO KNOW THE VALUE OF THE CARVINGS!!

SIDHU JETHA MAKES AN ENTRY. . . AGAIN.

HOT TEA FAST! HAVE YOU SEEN THE NEWS? TERRIBLE TRAGEDY!

THE FLIGHT FROM CALCUTTA TO KATHMANDU CRASHED AFTER TAKE OFF! ALL PASSENGERS DEAD INCLUDING US BANKER SILVERSTEIN!

WHERE DID IT CRASH?

NEAR SIDIKPUR VILLAGE ON THE HASNABAD ROAD. IT'S AN HOUR'S DRIVE FROM HERE.

IT'S THREE HOURS SINCE THE CRASH. WE HAVE TO LEAVE NOW. TOPSHE, MOVE!!

YESS SIR! I'LL GET READY!

FELUDA, CAN YOU FIND THE YAKSHI? THE POLICE AND THE FIRE BRIGADE MUST BE THERE ALREADY!!

WE HAVE TO TRY. LET'S GO!

FELUDA WHAT WILL YOU DO IF WE FIND THE YAKSHI?

GIVE IT TO THE ARCHAEOLOGICAL SURVEY OF INDIA. BUT WITH SILVERSTEIN DEAD I CAN'T CATCH THE THIEVES!

WE FOLLOWED THE MAN INTO THE APARTMENT BUILDING.

OH NO! HE'S GONE UP IN THE LIFT! WE HAVE LOST HIM FELUDA!

WE CAN STILL FIND OUT WHERE HE WENT...

WHEN THE LIFT CAME DOWN AGAIN...

WASN'T THAT MR SENGUPTA WHO WENT UP JUST NOW?

ARREY NAHIN! THAT WAS MALIK SAHIB OF FLAT NO.5.

OUR NEXT STOP WAS INSPECTOR DUTTA GUPTA'S OFFICE.

...SO THIS MALIK PROBABLY HAS THE YAKSHI. I'LL WATCH HIM AND IF YOU COULD CHECK HIM OUT TOO?

OKAY! GIVE ME ALL THE DETAILS. NAME? PLACE? DESCRIPTION?

MALIK STAYING IN FLAT NO. 5. QUEEN'S MANSION AND DRIVING A BLUE AMBASSADOR NO. WMA 5349. GOT IT!

MR MITTER, PLEASE BE CAREFUL! THESE ART THIEVES ARE DANGEROUS PEOPLE!

HUH! FELUDA KNOWS KARATE!

WE WENT BACK TO WATCH QUEEN'S MANSION AND THEN FOLLOWED MALIK TO NAGARMAL'S SHOP... VERY SUSPICIOUS!

WISH I COULD HEAR THEM!!

??!!

THEN HE WENT TO THE RAILWAY BOOKING OFFICE. I FOLLOWED HIM INSIDE. WHAT IS THE MAN UP TO?

INDIAN RAILWAYS
TICKETS

ONE SECOND CLASS AC TO AURANGABAD!

WHAT'S AT AURANGABAD?

FELUDA, HE BOUGHT A TICKET TO AURANGABAD. WHY?

I THINK WE HAVE TO CONSULT OUR ART EXPERT.

Y'MEAN SIDHU JETHA?

WE RUSH TO SIDHU JETHA'S HOUSE.

AURANGABAD!!?? THAT'S A DISASTER! DO YOU KNOW WHY HE IS GOING THERE?!

9

FROM AURANGABAD YOU GO TO ELLORA. WHERE THERE IS THE FAMOUS 8TH CENTURY KAILASH TEMPLE!

OH MY GOD! THAT CROOK MALIK'S PLANNING TO STEAL MORE CARVINGS AT ELLORA!!

PRECISELY SHERLOCK HOLMES JUNIOR!

BUT WHY IS HE GOING BY TRAIN?

HE WANTS TO KEEP THE YAKSHI WITH HIM. NO SECURITY CHECKS ON A TRAIN!

BACK HOME FELUDA DECIDED WE'LL FLY TO AURANGABAD.

JUPITER TRAVELS? I NEED THREE TICKETS TO AURANGABAD BY THE EARLIEST FLIGHT . . .

THREE? WHO?

ding dong!

HELLO! LALMOHAN BABU, ALIAS JATAYU! THE FAMOUS WRITER OF MYSTERY NOVELS!

HELLOOOO TAPESH BHAI! HOT SAMOSAS AND JALEBIS!

JATAYUJI START PACKING! THERE'S A MYSTERY AT HAND!

PHANTASTIC! PHABULOUS! SAMOSAS, JALEBIS AND A MYSTERY. I KNEW SOMETHING WAS UP! TELEPATHETIC OR WHAT?

TELEPATHIC!! OH PLEASE JATAYUJI! YOUR ENGLISH IS TOO MUCH!

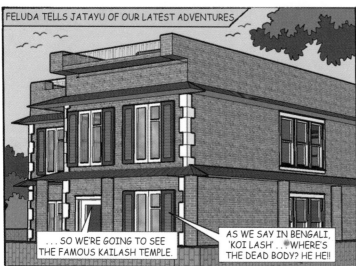

FELUDA TELLS JATAYU OF OUR LATEST ADVENTURES

. . . SO WE'RE GOING TO SEE THE FAMOUS KAILASH TEMPLE.

AS WE SAY IN BENGALI, 'KOI LASH' . . . WHERE'S THE DEAD BODY? HE HE!!

LATE THAT NIGHT A CALL . . .

MALIK CALLED BOMBAY FROM AN STD BOOTH. MY MAN WAS LISTENING. HE SAID, 'OUR DAUGHTER HAS COME HOME . . . HER FATHER IS TAKING HER TO 20-75'?!

20-75? OF COURSE! THAT'S A VERY CLEVER CODE!

BOMBAY IS A STRANGE CITY! WHY DO THEY CALL APOLLO A BANDAR, BHAI TAPESH? APOLLO THE MONKEY?!

JATAYU REALLY! BANDAR ALSO MEANS A PORT IN HINDI!

WHAT DID MALIK MEAN BY DAUGHTER COMING HOME?

SIMPLE! THE YAKSHI IS STILL WITH HIM, AT HOME IN INDIA!

AND TAKING HER TO 20-75? THAT CAN'T BE A DATE OR TIME!

STUDY THE MAP! THAT'S THE LATITUDE AND LONGITUDE OF AURANGABAD!

WHILE WAITING FOR OUR LUGGAGE AT AURANGABAD AIRPORT I MET SOMEONE . . .

YOU HAVE COME TO SEE ELLORA, YOUNG MAN?

YES. WE'RE STAYING AT THE AURANGABAD HOTEL.

GREAT! I'M ALSO STAYING THERE. I'M SHUBHANKAR BOSE. I TEACH HISTORY IN MICHIGAN AND AM WRITING A BOOK ON ELLORA.

OVER ICE CREAM SHAKES AT THE HOTEL COFFEE SHOP . . .

LOOK AT THIS! THIEVES HAVE STOLEN CARVINGS FROM A KHAJURAHO TEMPLE! THIS IS GETTING SERIOUS!

AGAIN? OH NO!

ART THIEVES STRIKE AGAIN!!!!!!

BOMBING

THE GANG HAS SPREAD ITS TENTACLES ACROSS INDIA. WE HAVE TO STOP THEM BEFORE MORE TEMPLES ARE RUINED.

WELL MALIK ONLY GETS HERE BY TRAIN TOMORROW.

Y'KNOW! I ALSO FIND THIS SHUBHANKAR BOSE CHAP MOST HIGHLY SUSPICIOUS! TOO FRIENDLY NO?

AND I FIND THIS DOUBLE SCOOP CHOCOLATE SENSATION SUSPICIOUSLY DELICIOUS LALMOHAN BABU!

WILL ANOTHER ICE CREAM HELP YOU THINK BETTER, DETECTIVES?

12

HELLO YOUNG MAN! SO YOU ARE READY FOR THE MAGIC OF ELLORA?

OH HELLO MR BOSE!

MEET MY COUSIN PRADOSH MITTER AND THIS IS LALMOHAN GANGULI ...

I AM HEH ... HEH ... A WRITER ...

OH REALLY! I'M ALSO WRITING A BOOK ON ELLORA. SO MAYBE WE CAN EXCHANGE NOTES.

THERE ARE SOME BEAUTIFUL BUDDHIST CAVES NEAR AURANGABAD. YOU SHOULDN'T MISS THEM. ALSO THERE IS THE BIBI KA MAQBARA WHICH AURANGZEB BUILT IN THE ... BLAH ... BLAH ... BLAH ... BLAH ...

THIS MAN CAN REALLY TALK! I'M FALLING ASLEEP ...

WE HAVE TO AVOID THIS MAN! I FIND HIM HIGHLY SUSPICIOUS. ANY MORE LECTURES ON HISTORY AND I'M GOING BACK TO CALCUTTA!

WE DECIDED TO TAKE A STROLL THROUGH THE STREETS OF AURANGABAD.

I'M A BIT PUZZLED FELUDA. IF MALIK HAS THE YAKSHI, WHY IS HE COMING TO AURANGABAD? HIS CUSTOMERS WOULD BE IN CITIES LIKE BOMBAY OR DELHI NO?

I'LL ONLY KNOW ONCE I FOLLOW MALIK AND SEE WHO HE IS MEETING HERE. I PLAN TO BE AT THE RAILWAY STATION WHEN HE ARRIVES.

ALSO WHILE HE IS HERE HE'LL PROBABLY TRY TO STEAL MORE CARVINGS. YOU HAVE TO STOP HIM FELU BABU!

IT WON'T BE EASY! THERE IS THE KAILASH TEMPLE AND DOZENS OF CAVES—HINDU, BUDDHIST, JAIN ... ALL FILLED WITH CARVINGS!

13

MALIK WOULD ARRIVE BY THE AFTERNOON TRAIN. SO WE WENT SIGHTSEEING NEXT MORNING.

THIS IS BIBI KA MAQBARA. THE TOMB OF AURANGZEB'S QUEEN RABIA-UD-DURRANI.

HMM . . . LOOKS SORT OF FAMILIAR!!

LIKE THE TAJ MAHAL WENT ON A DIET! HEE HEE HEE!

JATAYU IS STILL THINKING OF PROF. SHUBHANKAR BOSE . . .

??!!

CLICK

AT BOMBAY AIRPORT DURING CHECK IN I WAS BEHIND BOSE. HIS SUITCASE WEIGHED 35 KILOS! CAN YOU BELIEVE IT?

WHAT COULD HE BE CARRYING?

HAMMERS!! CHISELS!!

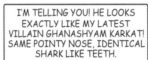

I'M TELLING YOU! HE LOOKS EXACTLY LIKE MY LATEST VILLAIN GHANASHYAM KARKAT! SAME POINTY NOSE, IDENTICAL SHARK LIKE TEETH.

HEY FELUDA, JATAYU SAYS PROF. BOSE'S LUGGAGE WEIGHED 35 KILOS.

CLICK!!

37 NOT 35. SO WHAT?

DON'T TELL BOSE YOU'RE A DETECTIVE! HE COULD BE DANGEROUS Y'KNOW!

WHAT'LL HE DO? HIT ME WITH HIS SUITCASE?

CLICK!!

OUTSIDE BIBI KA MAQBARA AS FELUDA WAS FEELING HUNGRY . . .

JATAYU THINKS HE'S CARRYING HAMMERS AND CHISELS TO BREAK THE CARVINGS.

NEWS TODAY

OR HE'S GOT BIG HEAVY ART BOOKS! CALM DOWN FOLKS! CHIPS ANYONE?

CRRUNCH . . . MALIK HAS THE YAKSHI HEAD REMEMBER? HE'LL HAVE THE HAMMER AND CHISEL . . . MUNCH . . . MUNCH . . . NOT BOSE!!

CHIPS

14

NEXT WE VISIT THE BUDDHIST CAVES AND HEY! WHO DO WE MEET THERE? THE SUSPICIOUS PROFESSOR!!

AHA! WELCOME TO THE FAMOUS BUDDHIST CAVES!

BOSE AGAIN? WHAT'S HE UP TO EH?

DON'T MISS NO.2 AND NO. 7 CAVES. WONDERFUL SCULPTURES THAT RESEMBLE AJANTA'S . . .

OOF! THIS MAN DOESN'T NEED A GUN! HE CAN KILL YOU BY BORING YOU!!

YOU TWO GO AHEAD! I HAVE TO SHOOT THIS . . . OOPS! SORRY!

LOOK WHERE YOU'RE GOIN' WILLYA?

STUPID FELLA! THESE CLUMSY INDIANS!

WE ESCAPED FROM BORING BOSE BY ENTERING A CAVE. IT WAS DARK INSIDE . . .

WOW! THIS IS SO COOL!

IMAGINE CARVING THAT FROM SOLID ROCK! YOU NEED SOLID MUSCLES BHAI!

OH GOOD! NO BOSE! LET'S SNEAK OFF FAST!

BUT WHERE'S FELUDA? MALIK IS ARRIVING BY THE AFTERNOON TRAIN! WE HAVE TO GO TO THE STATION NOW!

WE BEGAN TO SEARCH FOR FELUDA, WHO HAD VANISHED!

HELLOOO MISTER MITTER . . .

FELUDAAA! WHERE ARE YOU?

PROFESSOR HAVE YOU SEEN MY COUSIN?

NO. AND HE'S NOT IN THE CAVES EITHER! I'M COMING FROM THERE.

HE WAS HERE! LOOK!!

15

16

THEN MALIK ARRIVES WITH HIS FAMILIAR BAG.

I WAS WATCHING FROM THE LOBBY. THREE MEN ARRIVED, ALL LOOKING HIGHLY SUSPICIOUS!

ONE MAN LOOKS LIKE A HIPPY OR A HIPPO... WHATEVER YOU CALL 'EM. WHO'S THE ONE WITH THE BAG?

THAT'S OUR CROOK MALIK FROM CALCUTTA. HE'S GOT THE YAKSHI IN THE BAG!

I KNOW! AND WHY HAS FELUDA DISAPPEARED? WHAT'S HE UP TO?

AHA! NO WONDER. THAT'S WHY THE BAG WAS SO HEAVY! HE COULD HARDLY CARRY IT!

WHAT'S THAT? SOMEONE'S AT THE DOOR!

FINALLY A NOTE FROM FELUDA. THANK GOD.

HAVE LUNCH. PACK AND WAIT OUTSIDE AT 1.30 P.M. GET INTO TAXI NO. MHA 530. HAVE PAID HOTEL BILL.

IN THE RESTAURANT WE SAW PROF. BOSE AND MALIK LUNCHING TOGETHER, TALKING.

DOES BOSE KNOW THAT MALIK IS A CROOK? ...

LATER AS WE WAITED FOR OUR TAXI WHAT DO WE SEE?

LOOK! THEY ARE LEAVING FOR ELLORA TOO! I TOLD YOU TAPESH, THAT BOSE IS A CRIMINAL. IT'S THAT POINTY NOSE!

MISTER MITTER KA PARTY?

JI SARDARJI. WOH GREEN CAR KO FOLLOW KIJIYE!

GET IN QUICK! JATAYU IN FRONT!!

OOOF! BAAPREY!!

HEY!!

17

I KNOW THAT BAG!? FELUDA IT'S YOU!! THAT'S A REALLY COOL DISGUISE!

QUICK THINKING. SHABAASH TOPSHE!

??!!

OH WHAT A RELIEF! BUT WHY WAS FELUDA IN DISGUISE? HE EXPLAINS . . .

I WAS WORRIED MALIK WOULD RECOGNIZE ME. I SPOKE TO HIM REMEMBER? I WAS CARRYING THIS DISGUISE IN MY BAG AND CHANGED INSIDE A CAVE.

FROM THE CAVES I WENT TO THE STATION, PLANNING TO FOLLOW MALIK FROM THE STATION TO THE HOTEL. THEN I SHARED A TAXI WITH ANOTHER MAN TO COME TO THE HOTEL.

WE STOPPED ALONG THE WAY FOR HOT TEA AND SNACKS.

REMEMBER! I'M PIERCE MEETER A PHOTOGRAPHER FROM HONG KONG'S ASIA MAGAZINE. YOU'RE A HISTORY PROFESSOR. TOPSHE'S YOUR NEPHEW.

BUT I DON'T KNOW ANY HISTORY!

NOW LISTEN! THE KAILASH TEMPLE WAS BUILT IN THE 7TH CENTURY A.D. BY KING KRISHNA OF THE RASHTRAKUTA DYNASTY . . .

7TH CENTURY A.D. OR B.C.? KRISHNA . . . RIGHT! RASHTRAPATI . . . UMM NO . . . NO . . . RASHTRA . . . TOOKA? . . . I MEAN . . . OH HELL!

WASN'T THAT THE AMERICAN AND HIS WIFE? LOOKS LIKE EVERYONE'S GOING TO ELLORA!

WE SAW THE AMERICANS AT THE AURANGABAD CAVES REMEMBER?

ELLORA . . . KAILASH TEMPLE . . . HERE WE COME!

KHULDABAD'S THE NEAREST TOWN TO AJANTA AND ELLORA. ALONG THE WAY WE SAW THE FAMOUS CAVES CARVED OUT BY HAND AND FILLED WITH SCULPTURES AND PAINTINGS THIRTEEN CENTURIES AGO!

WHERE ARE YOU STAYING SIR? THE GUEST HOUSE OR THE DAK BUNGALOW?

AT THE BUNGALOW. THIS MUST BE THE GUESTHOUSE . . .

GREEN CAR! SO MALIK AND PROF. BOSE ARE STAYING HERE.

WE ARRIVE AT THE KHULADABAD DAK BUNGALOW

WE'LL LEAVE FOR KAILASH TEMPLE IN TEN MINUTES!

AND JATAYUJI PLEASE REMEMBER RASHTRAKUTA, 7TH CENTURY!!

AS WE WAITED FOR FELUDA WE SAW A FAMILIAR FACE.

NAMASKAR! YOU ARE BENGALIS LIKE ME?

???

YES SAR! STRAIGHT FROM CALCUTTA! I'M THE HISTORY OF . . . I MEAN PROFESSOR OF HISTORY, LALMOHAN GANGULI AND THIS IS MY NEPHEW TOP . . . NO . . . TAPESH!

HMMM . . . HOW INTERESTING!

I'M R.N. RAKSHIT FROM ALLAHABAD. I AM A LOVER AND COLLECTOR OF INDIAN ART.

I'M WRITING A BOOK ON ELLORA! A BOOK ON THE GREATEST WORK OF THE RASHTRAPOOTAS . . .

HE'S GETTING CONFUSED AGAIN! SHUT UP JATAYU!

POOR TOPSHE! NEEDS HELP!

OKAY GUYS! LET'S GO!

19

THE FABULOUS TEMPLE OF ELLORA. IT IS ONE OF THE TREASURES OF INDIAN ARCHITECTURE!

ANCIENT STONE CARVERS CHISELLED A SMALL HILL INTO A COMPLETE TEMPLE WITH IMAGES, HALLWAYS AND PILLARS!

WHAT AN AMAZING CREATION!!

IMAGINE! THEY BUILT THIS IN THE 7TH CENTURY! WE COULDN'T DO IT NOW! THEY CARVED A WHOLE HILL STARTING FROM THE TOP AND CUT-TING DOWNWARDS ...

MY GOD! IT'S JUST NOT SCULPTURE, IT'S GREAT ENGINEERING! HOW DID THEY DO IT?

MAYBE THIS WAS BUILT BY ALIENS FROM ANOTHER PLANET ... WOULDN'T THAT BE A GREAT PLOT WHAT?

SHHHHH ... SOMEONE'S COMING! QUICK! WALK AWAY FROM ME!

TAP ... TAP ... TAP ...

MALIK! HE WAS HERE BEFORE US. I WISH I KNEW WHAT HE WAS PLANNING ...

TAP ... TAP ... TAP ...

WELCOME TO THE WORLD FAMOUS KAILASH TEMPLE MR AND MRS LEWISON!

WELL ... I WAS PRETTY DISAPPOINTED WITH THOSE CAVES WE SAW YESTERDAY ...

I'VE SEEN BETTER CARVINGS IN THAILAND AND THE HOTELS IN BANGKOK ARE MUCH BETTER!

WHY WAS FELUDA SNAPPING PHOTOS OF BOSE, RAKSHIT AND THE LEWISONS?
DID HE SUSPECT THEM ALL?
I THOUGHT MALIK WAS THE THIEF!

CLICK! CLICK! CLICK! CLICK!

20

THERE WAS SO MUCH TO SEE AT THE KAILASH TEMPLE AND I REALIZED AN ART THIEF WOULD FIND A LOT TO STEAL.

OH HELLO! DID YOU FIND YOUR BROTHER THAT DAY?

ERR... UMM... YES! HE'S GONE TO BOMBAY FOR SOME URGENT WORK. HE'LL BE BACK SOON.

THAT MAN AGAIN!

HEY! WHAT ARE YOU DOING?

COOL IT MAN! I WAS JUST SHOOTING THAT PILLAR, NOT YOU!!

CLICK! CLICK!

RAKSHIT ARRIVED WITH THE LEWISONS. HE SEEMED TO KNOW THEM QUITE WELL.

EVERYONE'S HERE AT KAILASH. MALIK, BOSE, RAKSHIT, THE AMERICANS. WHO IS THE ART THIEF?

JATAYU AND I WENT BACK TO THE BUNGALOW. FELUDA LEFT FOR THE GUEST HOUSE.

LOOK! RAKSHIT'S FORGOTTEN TO LOCK HIS DOOR! SHALL WE SEARCH HIS ROOM?

YOU GO IN... I'LL KEEP WATCH OUTSIDE.

HMMM... SUITCASE LOCKED... INDIGESTION PILLS... TOOTHPASTE... NOTHING SUSPICIOUS. NO HAMMERS, NO GUNS!! HOW DISAPPOINTING!!

HANDS UP! THIS IS THE POLICE!!

??!!

MEANWHILE FELUDA INTRODUCES HIMSELF TO THE GUEST HOUSE MANAGER MR KULKARNI.

YOU'RE FAMOUS MR MITTER AND OF COURSE I'LL HELP! THE AMERICAN, MR LEWISON, IS AN ART COLLECTOR AND MR JAYANTO MALIK HAS ALREADY CALLED BOMBAY TWICE.

PLEASE LISTEN TO HIS CALLS NEXT TIME!

21

LOOK TAPESH! I ALWAYS FAILED IN HISTORY. I CAN'T REMEMBER ALL THIS RASHTRA-VASHTRA STUFF ... I HAVE A BRILLIANT PLAN!

snap!

I DISCOVERED LALMOHAN BABU'S PLAN AT DINNER.

SO WHICH PERIOD OF INDIAN HISTORY DO YOU SPECIALIZE IN PROFESSOR? RASHTRAKUTA?

EH? WHAT? EGYPT? NO ... NO ... I KNOW NOTHING ABOUT PYRAMIDS!

!?!

HEE HEE HEE! THAT'S SMART!

MY UNCLE IS VERY DEAF SIR AND HIS HEARING AID IS NOT WORKING!

OH? SO SAD!

AFTER DINNER, A STROLL AND WHO'S THAT COMING FROM THE GUEST HOUSE?

PROF. BOSE! WHERE'S HE GOING SO LATE AT NIGHT?

DO YOU KNOW THAT BENGALI CHAP IN THE BLUE SHIRT AND WHITE TROUSERS? JAYANTO MALIK?

THIS MAN GIVES ME A HEADACHE!

NO. DID HE SAY HE KNEW US?

PECULIAR CHAP! SAYS HE'S INTERESTED IN ART BUT HE DOESN'T KNOW ANY HISTORY. AND WHY'S HE GONE TO THE TEMPLE AT NIGHT?

HIGHLY SUSPICIOUS! ARE YOU FOLLOWING HIM??

EVEN THAT HIPPY PHOTOGRAPHER FELLOW LOOKS DANGEROUS!

HIPPY?! NO ... NO ... HE WORKS FOR A MAGAZINE IN CHUNG KING. TOTALLY HARMLESS CHAP ... HE ... HE ...

HONG KONG! OH PLEASE!

HE'S GOING TOWARDS THE KAILASH TEMPLE. WHO IS HE FOLLOWING? MALIK OR FELUDA??

22

NEXT MORNING WE WATCHED FELUDA GET INTO HIS DISGUISE. JATAYU HAD A BRAINWAVE...

CAN'T I GET A BEARD? OR A WIG? PLEASE FELU BABU! LIKE MY DETECTIVE PRAKHAR RUDRA?

NO WAY! TELL ME, HOW WILL YOU EXPLAIN GROWING A BEARD OR HAIR OVERNIGHT EH?

LATER, AS WE WALKED TOWARDS THE KAILASH TEMPLE WE SAW THE LEWISONS AGAIN WITH RAKSHIT, COMPLAINING AGAIN...

THE MOSQUITOES BITE SO BAAD! THE FOOD'S TERRIBLE! THE STUPID COOK CAN'T EVEN FRY AN EGG PROPERLY! WHATTA TERRIBLE COUNTRY!

HOW DO THEY FRY EGGS IN AMERICA, HMMM!!??

I SEE NO POINT IN OUR STAYING HERE ANY LONGER! I'M GOING BACK TO NEW YORK RIGHT NOW!

BUT MR LEWISON, YOU HAVEN'T SEEN AJANTA YET AND WHAT ABOUT...

WE DISCOVER THAT KAILASH TEMPLE HAD BEEN TAKEN OVER BY A FILM CREW FROM BOMBAY.

WHAT THE HELL! THIS IS AN ANCIENT TEMPLE. WHO ALLOWED THEM TO SHOOT HERE?

BUT WE CAN WATCH A FILM'S SHOOTING. WHAT SUPER DUPER FUN FELUDA!

EXCUSE ME! WHAT'S THE NAME OF THE FILM? WHO'S ACTING IN IT?

THE FILM IS *CROREPATI* WITH LEAD PAIR OF RUPA AND ARJUN MALHOTRA. THE VILLAIN IS BALWANT CHOPRA.

WOW! THAT'S A TOP CAST!!

IN THIS SCENE RUPA HAS BEEN KIDNAPPED AND KEPT IN THAT CAVE. THE HERO IS CHASING THE VILLAIN. AND THE CLIMAX SCENE? A FIGHT ON TOP OF THE TEMPLE!

FANTASTIC! THIS'LL BE A SUPER HIT!

WE WATCHED THE REHEARSAL OF A SCENE BETWEEN THE HEROINE AND THE VILLAIN

WHAT A SCREAM!

BACHAO! BACHAO!!

BASANTI AB TUM MERE KABZE MEIN HO! HA! HA! HA!!

EEEEEW!! HIS COLOGNE STINKS!

26

27

THE FILM SHOOTING HAD BEEN STOPPED. THE ACTRESS RUPA WAS HELPED AWAY AND WE HEARD THE POLICE WAS COMING . . .

DID HE SAY DEAD BODY? THIS LOOKS SERIOUS. I WONDER WHAT'S HAPPENED?

I'LL GO AND ASK THE COSTUME GIRL.

I DON'T KNOW . . . A MAN'S DEAD BODY IS LYING IN THE DITCH BEHIND THE TEMPLE. BUT HE'S NOT FROM THE FILM CREW.

??!!

DON'T GO THERE! IT'S A HORRIBLE SIGHT. POOR MAN!

I HAVE TO SEE WHO IT IS. YOU TWO WAIT FOR ME HERE . . .

OH MY GOD! IT'S PROF. SHUBHANKAR BOSE! HOW DID HE DIE?

LAST NIGHT I SAW HIM CLIMBING THAT HILL BEHIND THE TEMPLE. I TOLD HIM IT WAS DANGEROUS. HE DIDN'T LISTEN!

IMAGINE COMMITTING SUICIDE IN THIS WAY! COMING TO ELLORA AND THEN JUMPING OFF A HILL? WAS THE MAN MAD?

SUICIDE? HOW CAN YOU BE SURE?

THIS IS NOT AN ACCIDENT. HE'S BEEN HIT ON THE HEAD FROM BEHIND AND THEN PUSHED INTO THE DITCH. WHAT'S THAT IN HIS HAND?

MEANWHILE THE FILM DIRECTOR DECIDED TO CANCEL THE SHOOTING.

NO SHOOTING TODAY! PACK UP!!

28

HELLO MR KULKARNI. HAVE YOU HEARD THE NEWS?

INSPECTOR GHOTE OF THE KHULDABAD POLICE CALLED ME THIS MORNING. WHAT A TRAGEDY SIR!

THIS MORNING I DISCOVERED PROF. BOSE WAS MISSING FROM HIS ROOM. NOW INSPECTOR GHOTE HAS GONE TO CHECK THE BODY . . .

WILL YOU INTRODUCE ME TO GHOTE? I HAVE SOME IMPORTANT INFORMATION FOR HIM.

CERTAINLY! BY THE WAY, MALIK CALLED BOMBAY AGAIN. HE SAID HIS DAUGHTER IS FINE. ALSO HE WANTED TO LEAVE TODAY.

NO WAY! WE HAVE TO STOP HIM!

I'VE ALREADY DONE THAT MR MITTER! I TOLD HIM THAT HIS CAR HAD GONE FOR REPAIRS AND IT WILL TAKE ALL DAY.

BRILLIANT KULKARNI SAHIB!!

YOU TWO GO BACK TO THE BUNGALOW AND WAIT FOR ME!

THERE'S INSPECTOR GHOTE. COME ALONG SIR!

ENTER INSPECTOR GHOTE!!!

THEN KULKARNI INTRODUCED FELUDA TO A HAPPY LOOKING INSPECTOR GHOTE OF KHULDABAD POLICE.

THE FAMOUS DETECTIVE PRADOSH MITTER!

OH MY! A PRIVATE EYE!! A CLEVER SPOOK WHO'LL CATCH A CROOK!! WHAT AN HONOUR HE HE . . . TO MEET YOU!

A POLICEMAN WHO LOOKS LIKE A FAT CHARLIE CHAPLIN AND TELLS AWFUL JOKES! WHAT NEXT?

BACK AT THE BUNGALOW WE WENT BACK TO OUR ROOM AND JATAYU MADE A DISCOVERY . . .

TAPESH, WHEN WE LEFT IN THE MORNING, DID WE LEAVE THE DOOR OPEN?

NO. I CLOSED IT BUT IT WASN'T LOCKED. WHY?

30

THANK YOU MR KULKARNI. GOODBYE!

KYA?! WHY NOT STAY FOR A FEW DAYS LONGER SIR?

MR. LEWISON! WAIT A MOMENT PLEASE!

WHAT IS THAT CROOK MALIK UP TO? IS HE RUNNING AWAY?

MY CAR'S GONE FOR REPAIRS. CAN I TAKE A LIFT TO THE RAILWAY STATION WITH YOU?

SURE! C'MON. LET'S GO!

OH HO! HE'S LEAVING. I HAVE TO CONTACT MR MITTER IMMEDIATELY!

MEANWHILE FELUDA WAS TELLING INSPECTOR GHOTE THE WHOLE STORY.

WE HAVE TO MAKE SURE THAT THE LEWISONS AND MALIK DO NOT LEAVE ELLORA!

I'LL SEND MY MEN TO KEEP WATCH AT THE RAILWAY STATION.

I CAN'T KEEP UP WITH THEIR CAR ON THIS OLD BIKE!...HUFF...PUFF HAVE TO FIND FELUDA!

MEANWHILE AT THE GUEST HOUSE KULKARNI TRIED TO DELAY MALIK.

ONE MOMENT SIR! I HAVE TO PREPARE YOUR BILL.

HURRY UP MAN! I'LL MISS MY TRAIN!

32

I'LL LISTEN TO YOUR STORY AT THE POLICE STATION MR MALIK. RIGHT NOW YOU ARE UNDER ARREST FOR THE THEFT OF INDIAN ANTIQUES!

NOW WAIT A MOMENT! WHAT ABOUT US? WE WERE JUST GIVING THIS MAN A LIFT. CAN YOU UNDERSTAND THAT?

WE HAVE A PLANE TO CATCH IN BOMBAY. GET IT?

I HAVE NO EVIDENCE AGAINST YOU! YOU TWO CAN LEAVE.

WHAT EVIDENCE? WE ARE NOT CRIMINALS! WE ARE TOURISTS! 'BYE!!

I'M PRETTY SURE THEY WERE HERE TO BUY STOLEN INDIAN ANTIQUES.

OOOF! WHAT A DAY! FIRST RIDING A CYCLE WITH THAT CRAZY TAPESH. THEN A JEEP DRIVEN BY A LUNATIC POLICEMAN! IT'S A MIRACLE I'M STILL ALIVE!!

YOU KNOW MR MITTER THOSE AMERICANS WERE VERY SUSPICIOUS. THEY WERE DEFINITELY LOOKING FOR STOLEN CARVINGS.

BUT THERE WAS NO EVIDENCE. WHAT COULD YOU DO?

MALIK WAS TAKEN AWAY TO THE KHULDABAD POLICE STATION.

DO PLEASE CHECK THE TELEPHONE NUMBERS THAT MALIK WAS CALLING IN BOMBAY MR GHOTE.

WILL DO. NOW OUR JOB IS TO CATCH THE WHOLE GANG!

ENDS WELL THAT ALL'S WELL! WHAT TAPESH RANJAN?

ERRR . . . LALMOHAN BABU IT IS 'ALL'S WELL THAT ENDS WELL'!

34

INSPECTOR GHOTE, CAN I KEEP THE YAKSHI FOR ONE DAY?

YES OF COURSE. BUT WHY DO YOU NEED IT? NOW THAT MALIK'S BEEN ARRESTED THE CASE IS SOLVED, NO?

NOPE! THE CASE IS NOT OVER YET. THE KINGPIN OF THE GANG IS STILL MISSING!

OH MAN! YOU MEAN MALIK IS NOT THE GANG LEADER?

NOW THAT MALIK'S BEEN CAUGHT I'M GOING TO TAKE OFF MY DISGUISE. BUT REMEMBER! YOU TWO DON'T KNOW ME! WE CATCH THE REAL CROOKS TONIGHT!

REAL CROOKS?!

FELUDA HAD VANISHED AGAIN. SO LALMOHAN BABU AND I WENT TO HAVE LUNCH WHEN SUDDENLY . . .

HAVE YOU ANY NEWS ABOUT THE MURDER?

HELLO!!

ENTER FELUDA AS HIMSELF AGAIN. JATAYU AND I STAY VERY QUIET.

I HEAR THEY HAVE CAUGHT A MAN STEALING CARVINGS FROM KAILASH?

A THIEF HAS BEEN CAUGHT? OH REALLY? I DIDN'T KNOW . . .

IN THE EVENING THERE'S ANOTHER NOTE FROM FELUDA.

Go to cave no. 15 at 7 p.m. Hide on the upper floor.

THAT EVENING AT 6.45 P.M. CAVE NO 15. IT WAS THE DASAVATARA CAVE WHERE WE SAW THE TORCHLIGHT THE NIGHT BOSE DIED.

TAPESH I'M FEELING TOTALLY NERVOUS BHAI! LOOK! MY HANDS ARE SHAKING . . . MY POOR HEART IS . . .

WE WENT TO THE UPPER FLOOR AND HID BEHIND A PILLAR.

I WISH I HAD A GUN LIKE FELUDA!

GUN?! OH NO!! MAA KALI HELP MEEEE!!

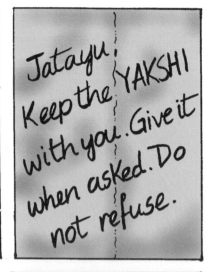

MALIK CATCHING RAKSHIT! I THOUGHT HE WAS BEHIND BARS. WHAT'S HAPPENING?

MEET JAYANTO MALIK. HE IS A PRIVATE INVESTIGATOR LIKE ME. HE WAS ALSO TRYING TO SAVE THE YAKSHI.

JUST LIKE SIDHU JETHA, MALIK ALSO SAW SOL SILVERSTEIN WITH THE YAKSHI AT NAGARMAL'S SHOP AT THE GRAND HOTEL IN CALCUTTA.

THIS IS A GENUINE CARVING FROM ORISSA SIR. VERY OLD, INDEED!

AWESOME! PRETTY ISN'T SHE?

I ALSO WENT TO SIDIKPUR BUT RAKSHIT GOT THERE FIRST. I FOLLOWED HIS CAR BUT ON THE WAY MY CAR GOT A FLAT TYRE.

WHAT MADE YOU SUSPECT RAKSHIT?

LAST NIGHT WHEN I SEARCHED THE CAVE I FOUND HIS RAINCOAT HIDDEN BEHIND A PILLAR.

INSIDE A SPECIALLY MADE POCKET I FOUND A HAMMER AND CHISEL.

BY THE TIME WE LEFT THE KAILASH TEMPLE, DAWN WAS BREAKING. RAKSHIT WAS TAKEN AWAY BY THE POLICE AND WE HEADED BACK TO THE DAK BUNGALOW.

I SUSPECTED TWO PEOPLE. RAKSHIT AND THAT STRANGE PHOTOGRAPHER FROM HONG KONG. I KNEW HE WAS IN DISGUISE.

LUCKY I TOOK OFF THE BEARD AND WIG! OR YOU WOULD HAVE HAD ME ARRESTED HE HE . . .

BUT THEN HOW DID YOU FIND THE YAKSHI?

LAST NIGHT WHEN RAKSHIT WENT OUT, I TOOK IT FROM HIS ROOM. I DIDN'T KNOW HE WAS PLANNING TO STEAL AGAIN. LUCKY FELU BABU SCARED HIM OFF BY THROWING THAT PEBBLE AT THE CAVE.

AHHA! SO THAT WAS WHAT HE WAS SEARCHING FOR THAT NIGHT! HE TOLD ME IT WAS BATS!

39

## SATYAJIT RAY (1921 – 1992)

Satyajit Ray was considered one of the greatest film directors of the twentieth century. He directed 37 films, including two on Feluda's adventures. He also wrote the scripts, composed the music, operated the camera, designed the sets and edited the films! Ray was awarded an Oscar, the Academy of Motion Pictures Award for Lifetime Achievement in 1992.

At the same time Ray was editing a Bengali children's magazine called *Sandesh*, where he wrote, designed the cover and drew amazing illustrations. It was in the pages of *Sandesh* that in 1965 he created a detective called Feluda, who became an instant hit with the children of Bengal. He also wrote a science fiction series around a scientist called Professor Shonku.

A Feluda mystery often takes him, his cousin Topshe and friend Jatayu to magical places like Jaisalmer, Kathmandu and Hong Kong. With fascinating plots the stories are also full of interesting information about places, as also cryptic puzzles, puns and word games. Ray wrote 35 Feluda stories full of mystery and action, puzzling crimes and dangerous crooks and always Feluda wins the game!

## SUBHADRA SEN GUPTA

Subhadra's books for children include mysteries, historical and ghost stories. What she loves the most is writing the scripts for comics that Tapas illustrates. She enjoys writing about interesting places, weird people, music, cats and good food. Start a conversation with her by emailing to: subhadrasg@gmail.com.

## TAPAS GUHA

Tapas is a well-known illustrator who loves dreaming up comic strips. As a kid he taught himself to draw by studying the illustrations of comics like Tintin, Phantom, Mandrake and of course Satyajit Ray. You can see samples of his work at: www.tapasguha.com or write to him at tapsguha@gmail.com.

A sudden violent storm takes Kolkata by surprise. It also leaves Narendra Nath Biswas injured, hit by a falling tree in the Park Street Cemetery . . . or was it the work of some unknown assailant? Feluda starts his own investigations and soon encounters enough questions to puzzle his matchless intellect.

Who was Thomas Godwin and why
is someone digging up his grave?
What is a Perigal Repeater?
Who is this mysterious N.M. Biswas?

In his search for answers, Feluda digs up the fascinating history of the Godwin family, going back to nineteenth-century Lucknow and learns about Thomas Godwin's precious heirloom. Ghostly happenings in a graveyard, a ruthless criminal with a gang of thugs, a master chef and a happy guitar player come together in an adventure full of danger and excitement.

SATYAJIT RAY'S FELUDA MYSTERIES

DANGER IN
DARJEELING

ART: TAPAS GUHA
SCRIPT: SUBHADRA SEN GUPTA

Lalmohan Babu is in Bollywood! The best-selling mystery writer's novel is being made into a Hindi film and the location for the shoot is the hill station of Darjeeling. Feluda, Topshe and Lalmohan Babu arrive in Darjeeling to watch the film being made, where they meet the mysterious Virupaksha Majumdar, a man with many secrets and a precious gold idol. When Virupaksha is murdered and the idol stolen, Feluda knows the answer lies in his past. Then Topshe and Lalmohan Babu discover a second body and things get very complicated. To make matters worse, one misty morning a shadowy figure viciously attacks Feluda.

As the trio races against time, can they solve three perplexing crimes? One of Feluda's most exciting and thrilling cases comes alive in this newest addition to the popular comic book series.

The trail of a murder in a hotel in Kolkata takes Feluda, Topshe and Lalmohan Babu to the beautiful city of Kathmandu in Nepal. Here in the Himalayas the mystery deepens. A man claims he has a double, a crook who looks exactly like him. Then there is the tragic death of a helicopter pilot who discovered a nefarious smuggling ring. The intrepid trio faces danger amidst the busy bazaars, temples and stupas of Kathmandu and Lalmohan Babu has a scary, out-of-body experience.

Finally Feluda comes face to face with his greatest adversary, a ruthless villain who will stop at nothing . . .